Wind

Look for the other books on weather by

Marion Dane Bauer
Snow • Rain • Clouds

ALADDIN PAPERBACKS
An imprint of Simon & Schuster Children's Publishing Division
1230 Avenue of the Americas
New York, NY 10020

Book design by Debra Sfetsios
The text of this book was set in Century Schoolbook.

Printed in Mexico

ISBN 0-689-85443-9 (pbk.) — ISBN 0-689-85442-0 (library ed.)

Wind

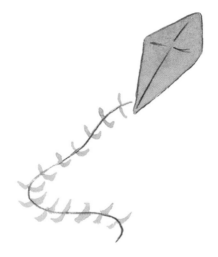

written by Marion Dane Bauer

illustrated by John Wallace

Aladdin
New York London Toronto Sydney Singapore

The earth we live on
is a spinning ball.

When the earth spins,
the air around it
moves too.

When air moves,
we call it "wind."
As the sun heats the air,
the air grows lighter.
Light air rises.

Cool air is heavy.
It falls.

Cool air and warm air
are always trading places.

We call this movement
"wind."

Birds use wind
to help them fly.

Plants use wind
to carry their seeds.

We use wind
to fly kites,

to sail boats,

and to turn
windmills.

Wind moves clouds.
Wind makes waves.
It even makes trees bend.

When the hot air
is very light
and the cold air
is very heavy,
wind can blow up a storm!

Sometimes wind spins
like a puppy
chasing its tail.

A small spin
makes a dust devil
or a water spout.

A strong spin
makes a tornado
or a hurricane.

Wind can be scary.

Or it can sing
a gentle song.

Wind is all around us,
but we cannot see it.

We can only see
what wind does.

Facts about wind:

The air that surrounds the Earth is called the troposphere. It is only about eight miles deep.

The hardest gust of wind ever measured was on Mount Washington. It was 231 miles per hour.

When wind blows snow very hard, we have a blizzard.

The eye of a hurricane is still. The winds are quiet there. After the eye passes, the winds blow in the opposite direction.